One and a half miles wide with
winds up to two hundred miles per hour.

Turn on the sirens,
and *leave* them on!

For Edward,
with love
from Dad

Farrar Straus Giroux Books for Young Readers
175 Fifth Avenue, New York 10010

Copyright © 2016 by Allan Drummond
All rights reserved
Color separations by Bright Arts (H.K.) Ltd.
Printed in China by Toppan Leefung Printing Ltd.,
Dongguan City, Guangdong Province
First edition, 2016
1 3 5 7 9 10 8 6 4 2

mackids.com

Library of Congress Cataloging-in-Publication Data

Drummond, Allan, author.
    Green city : how one community survived a tornado and rebuilt for
a sustainable future / Allan Drummond. — First edition.
        pages   cm
    Summary: "The story of Greensburg, Kansas, a town that rebuilt
completely green after a deadly tornado"—Provided by publisher.
    ISBN 978-0-374-37999-5 (hardback)
    1. Sustainability—Kansas—Greensburg—Juvenile literature.
    2. Sustainable living—Kansas—Greensburg—Juvenile literature.
    3. Green movement—Kansas—Greensburg—Juvenile literature.
    4. Tornadoes—Kansas—Greensburg—Juvenile literature.
    5. Greensburg (Kan.)—Juvenile literature.   I. Title.

GE195.5.D78 2016
640.28'6—dc23

2015018065

Our books may be purchased in bulk for promotional, educational, or
business use. Please contact your local bookseller or the Macmillan
Corporate and Premium Sales Department at (800) 221-7945 ext. 5442
or by e-mail at MacmillanSpecialMarkets@macmillan.com.

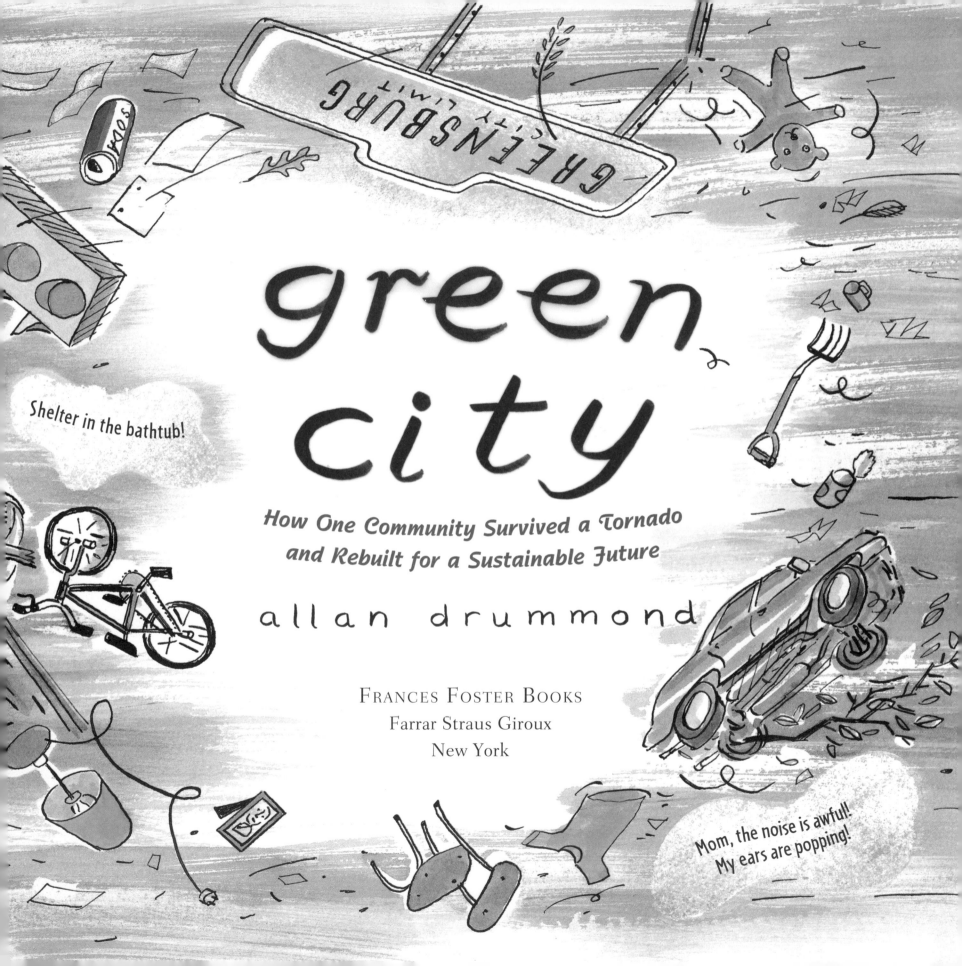

GREENSBURG CITY LIMIT

green city

How One Community Survived a Tornado and Rebuilt for a Sustainable Future

allan drummond

FRANCES FOSTER BOOKS
Farrar Straus Giroux
New York

Shelter in the bathtub!

Mom, the noise is awful!
My ears are popping!

I remember the night when a tornado destroyed Greensburg in nine minutes flat.

All of my things, our house, *everything* was blown thousands of feet into the air.

When it was all over and we climbed out of our shelter in the basement, everyone's past had been swept away.

Suddenly the entire town of Greensburg had no future.

Eleven people died because of the storm.

It took twelve people to lift a truck off Mr. Schmidt's house.

It was like a huge bomb had gone off. Our school was destroyed just two weeks before graduation.

The hospital, nine churches, the water tower, the drugstore with its soda fountain, the grocery store, the two hotels, the three banks, the theater, and everything else—just gone.

The trees were shredded to nothing. Not a bird in sight.

The only buildings left standing were the courthouse, the historic S.D. Robinett building,

and Greensburg's giant grain elevator complex.

And looking at the town from high up, it was clear that nothing was left.
Some people were asking, "What good is Greensburg anymore?"
After all, we'd only been a little town in the middle of endless cornfields.

Down on the ground there was a gigantic mess to clean up.

The very next day we met in a huge emergency tent set up amid rubble outside the courthouse. Five hundred people were there, along with TV news teams, emergency crews, and volunteers.

With almost no buildings left, the only thing that remained of Greensburg was the people.

Everyone set to work.

The president flew in and declared Greensburg a disaster area.

So many volunteers flocked to the town we had to build a whole trailer park for them!

GOD BLESS GREENSBURG

Thanks to ♥ ALL ♥ VOLUNTEERS

Donations came from all over Kansas, the United States, and the world.

The government sent experts to help us.

And there was a whole lot of rubble to clear out—more than 388,000 tons.

We had to move out of town and find somewhere to stay during the big cleanup.

By the summer, we were living in our own small city of three hundred trailer homes outside Greensburg.

Life was not easy, and there were disagreements. Some people moved away and never came back.

Out there, living close to the weather, we realized how hot Kansas really could be.

We had to drive everywhere.

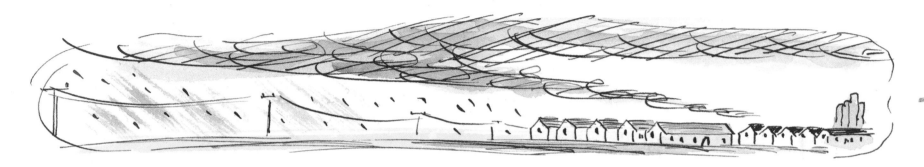

And there was always the chance that our trailers would be blown away by the wind.

We kept dreaming of what Greensburg and our new homes would look like.

We did a lot of talking about how to build again.

Sure, we all agreed on tornado-proof houses. And houses that we could keep cool in the summer and warm in the winter without using more fuel than necessary would be great. The word *green* kept coming up at every meeting.

"Isn't green just a color of paint?" asked Bob Dixson.

Then Daniel Wallach spoke up. "Green is basic common sense," he declared. "Don't use up more than you need. It's sustainability! The Kansas farmers' way!"

Mr. Wallach opened an office and called it Greensburg GreenTown.

"Not just green houses, a whole green city!" he said.

The whole idea of a green city had everyone excited, and some people got really creative. Lana and John Janssen reclaimed the kitchen cabinets and tiles from the remnants of their old house.

Daniel Wallach suggested the Silo Eco-Home, with rounded walls like the grain elevator complex that survived the storm.

Jill and Scott Eller started work on an amazing wind-resistant geodesic dome home made from wooden panels.

Bob Dixson designed a super-strong, super-insulated wood frame for his home.

Sixteen sustainable, affordable houses, called the Prairie Pointe Townhomes, would be built for Greensburgers right on Main Street.

But these were difficult times, and not everyone had the money to keep going.

My family was lucky, and for the next two years we worked hard to build our home in as sustainable a way as possible.

BUILDING A SUSTAINABLE HOUSE

1. A house loses heat through its windows. The cold north side of a house gets little or no sun, so the windows should be smaller here. The rooms that aren't used much during the day should be put on the cold side.

2. The sunny south side of a house can have large windows to allow the light and warmth of the sun into the dwelling.

3. Solar pipes made of shiny metal with a clear cover on top can be set into the roof to bring sunlight down into dark areas, reducing the need for electric light during the day.

4. Plenty of insulation in the walls, roof, and floor of a house acts like a warm blanket, keeping the heat inside. All this insulation keeps the house cool in summer, too.

5. Solar panels generate electricity from the sun.

6. Water use can be reduced with special faucets and toilets.

7. Reclaimed materials can be used to build new floors and walls.

8. Sometimes appliances and cabinets can be reclaimed, too.

9. Rainwater can be collected from the roof and used to water the garden.

10. Some types of plants require less water.

11. Light-colored sidewalks and paths are much cooler to walk on than dark ones. They reflect the heat of the sun.

The town's businesses were rebuilding green, too—new offices for start-up companies, and a retail center.

The 5.4.7 Arts Center arrived by truck and was put together by University of Kansas architecture students.

On the outskirts of town we built a wind farm big enough to power the whole community.

The banks made sure their new buildings were as eco-friendly as possible.

So did the Best Western hotel and, beside it, the Kiowa County Memorial Hospital.

Our new hurricane-proof water tower was constructed next to the new, green Big Well Museum.

We knew our school had to be at the very center of it all.
The plans looked exciting.

For three years we only had small trailers for classrooms.

But we became experts in environmental science.

THE KIOWA COUNTY SCHOOL LEADS THE WAY IN GREEN SCHOOL DESIGN

The Kiowa County School was designed to be the greenest building in the whole town. It was built from scratch. Reclaimed and recycled materials were used wherever possible, and the school has a wind turbine to generate electricity. Insulation in the roof, walls, and floors makes the building very energy efficient, and a special ground source heat-pump system means the school requires no fuel for heating. Classrooms are positioned to use the warmth and light from the sun. All the faucets and toilets use as little water as possible, and rain is collected on the roof and used to water the landscape.

Our new school was going to be one of the
greenest in the United States.

It took a few years for everything to come together, but now look! Greensburg is Green City.

We moved into our new houses, and Greensburg has finally come back to life.

I still remember the night when the tornado destroyed our town in nine minutes flat.

Back then it really did seem like the end for Greensburg. Our town and our future were shattered.

But we *did* rebuild into one of the greenest towns in America.

That's official—the president even said so on TV.

"A global example of how clean energy can power an entire community."

By thinking and building green, we've given Greensburg its future. We planned for the future, because the future *is* green. Just ask the experts!

BUILDING BETTER FOR THE FUTURE

Better means green, and green means common sense!

AUTHOR'S NOTE

Greensburg calls itself a city, but in fact it is a small community. About 1,400 people lived there before the terrible tornado of May 4, 2007. Since then, the city has been transformed by hard work, dedication, and a focus on going green. But still, the population of Greensburg is much smaller—now only about eight hundred residents. For some people, the challenge of rebuilding a home or a business, or getting back to normal family life, meant that moving away and starting afresh was the best answer.

For those who stayed, rebuilding was not just about repairing and constructing new buildings; it was also about making a town that people would want as a lifelong home. Job opportunities with new businesses and educational opportunities with the town's school are an important part of Greensburg's long-term recovery plan. Even years later, Greensburg still faces economic struggles and is working toward a full recovery, but its residents' dedication to a new and sustainable lifestyle has shown that it truly deserves to be called America's Green City.

As I started work on this book, my own family's house suffered from a devastating fire. Fortunately nobody was hurt. Neighbors and friends rushed to help us, but the house was destroyed, and we were left with difficult choices. Should we stay and take on the challenge of rebuilding? Or should we move? We chose to rebuild, and to make our house as green as possible. Suddenly we found ourselves living through the same challenges I was writing about and illustrating. Energy, sunlight, insulation, heating, water, building materials, transport costs—everything to do with making a sustainable building—became real to us. Now we, too, have a house built for the future.